HUMANITY'S CONUNDRUM

Why is Homo Sapiens both gifted with such reason,
and yet cursed with such turbulent restlessness?

Why do we suffer? And how do we heal?

A parable: an alternative psychology

By David Zigmond

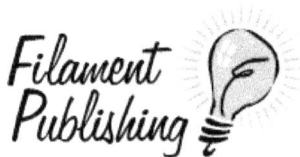

Published by
Filament Publishing Ltd.
16 Croydon Road, Beddington
Croydon, Surrey, CR0 4PA, United Kingdom
www.filamentpublishing.com
Telephone: +44 (0)208 688 2598

ISBN 978-1-913192-73-0
Printed by 4edge Ltd

Testimonials

" David Zigmond lays out a deceptively simple, but profound, analysis of the source of much mental suffering in humanity – an outsize brain with excess capacity to envisage 'what is not' – which can run away with itself. This little book is a profoundly human and humanising resource, which could provide clarity and hope for a very wide readership. "

John Sloboda, Emeritus Professor of Psychology,
Keele University

" David Zigmond has written something important, timely and deep, stressing human connection in the process of healing emotional and psychological pain. His integrative approach places as much importance on society as the individual.

Profound and accessible at the same time: no mean feat. It's a comforting and inspiring read, universalising our difficulties. I could see myself in there – and in that sense, everyone. "

Jan Woolf, author of Fugues on a Funny Bone *and* Stormlight

" Some undeniable and uncomfortable truths from an original and provocative thinker. This deserves to be read by both anguished and their comforters and guides alike. "

Gaie Houston, Veteran psychotherapist and author

" I haven't come across such pithy philosophy since *The Socratic Dialogues* and that was more than 2,000 years ago… Seriously, I have never read a book by a shrink before, but at least I now know why I behave like I do! "

Ken Livingstone, Ex-Mayor of London and MP

" [David Zigmond] brings a sharp focus to produce this masterpiece of a monograph that cuts through an academic and administrative jungle.

This magnificent small book, in its brevity, playfully and pithily re-views our thoughts, feelings and behaviours in a way that demystifies psychotherapy and so makes it accessible to all who are curious enough to understand.
The uniqueness of this writing is how its rich breadth is expressed with such serious but humorous clarity… As soon as I read this book many things fell into place for me, rather belatedly in my career.

… provides such a valuable framework for understanding ourselves, and then offers us an optimistic view as to how we humans can help, instead of obstruct or torment, ourselves and others… That, surely, is worth our time and attention. 〞

Emeritus Professor Sue Wheeler, University of Leicester

〝 This is a delightful and insightful book. It describes the problem of being human and tackles the profound questions of life, love and death; linking our existential anxiety to having a large brain with spare capacity. David Zigmond finds the remedies for the human condition not only from his work as a GP, Psychiatrist and Psychotherapist but also from a long life of being a thoughtful and compassionate human being human. 〞

Pauline Hodson, Psychotherapist, author of The Business of Therapy – How to Run a Successful Private Practice *and* The Invisible Matrix.

〝 At last Socrates and Jean-Paul Sartre come together in the form of David Zigmond producing first rate dialogical existentialism. Doing talking therapy can be a mysterious activity: Zigmond's book not only honours that mystery, but does so with an unusual mixture of solid seriousness and playful wit. If that appeals, then this book is definitely the one to reach for.. 〞

Robin Hobbes, Ethical Advisor to The European Transactional Analysis Association

Contents

Prelude: post-scripted intra-Covid

How do you make God laugh?
Tell Him your future plans.
– Woody Allen

As happened with innumerable human projects early in 2020, the launch of this book, *Humanity's Conundrum*, too, was scuppered by Covid-19: our now ubiquitous stymie and burden. This invisible and previously unknown foe has since changed everyone's life beyond our familiar capacities to plan or to imagine.

Yet this period – so perilously bewildering and frustrating for so many – has also served as a kind of philosophical space – frequently involuntary – for us to ask fundamental questions of ourselves. As a society we must grapple with how much life should we stop to possibly stop some death? Who should decide this and how? Individually many of us are asking: what and who is most important to us? Why do we need others, and what for? Why are we so inconsistent, often seeking strange and changing mixtures of closeness and distance, and then in turn, the bracingly novel and the comfortingly familiar? And how do we wish to include other, non-human, life forms in these questions? These individual-yet-universal questions fuel much of the material of this book.

At the time of writing, now several months into our unpredictable communal seclusion, many people describe curious paradoxes: amidst the fear, they feel reassured by rediscovering neglected values; in lonely isolation, they sense and witness a shared human travail and predicament. Not all, of course. For some, the pain and deprivation of social distancing and dislocation far exceeds any fruit-fall of rekindled meaning or epiphany of life's blessings: statisticians then present us with grim data of increased rates of domestic violence, mental breakdown and suicides.

*

In the first week of our lockdown period, while taking some early morning spring sunshine, fresh air and exercise, I approached a similarly aged man on the largely deserted street. We automatically manoeuvred a large avoidance-arc around one another, implicitly recognising this new Covid-era of stranger-danger, the other as harbinger of harm.

He called out, 'Strange times, eh?'

Keeping my two-metre protection distance I said, 'They sure are, and we don't know for how long…'

'Well that's like life, isn't it? What do we really know?', he chuckled, 'but we're certainly still here, for now anyway … and what a beautiful morning!', he said, his gaze first cast skyward and then lowering to hold mine with a smile. I sensed then a warmth that extended to a fleeting but deep intimacy – a knowing fraternalism that was both melancholic and sweet. In those few moments we merged, I believe, into a tender sharing of that vast unmasterable hinterland – the hauntings of mortality, aloneness and so our never-ending task of making sense and connections … our bridges to one another and all that is not-self.

As I turned aside from this rich yet brief encounter, I thought how it had – with so little time or words – captured the essence of *Humanity's Conundrum.*

If you read this book you will discover how capricious and serendipitous was its conception, how it was first fertilised by eccentrically light events. In contrast, the later 'birth' of the book – its planned physical launch – is quite the opposite: deliberately conceived and carefully designed, it was fated instead to be miscarried by much larger, grimmer, now global forces. Indeed, we are all currently witnessing how the most primitive life-form (Are viruses alive? Discuss…) is threatening the viability of the unequalled, certainly unprecedented, complexity of contemporary human life: our ever-denser and larger, more mobile populations living in previously unimaginably large conurbations; our utter dependence on complex mass-productions and hi-tech cybernation; our striving for an eternal growth economy that marshals hegemony over all other life… All of these – we have come to presume – can then bestow on us humans an ever-increasing stream of choices, powers and gratifications…

All of this is now suddenly stalled – at the very least – by the primordial genius of a virus. The indefinite deferral of the physical launch of *Humanity's Conundrum* is a small matter of largely personal significance, but the hiatus in which that has occurred has brought to the fore many of the questions the book explores. However we emerge from Covid these questions will remain timeless, crucial and inescapable.

David Zigmond, February 2021

Foreword

Why do we suffer?
And how do we heal?

These may be the two most innocently profound questions we ask of ourselves and others. In *Humanity's Conundrum*, David Zigmond uses them as stepping stones to explore the familiar yet endlessly troubling predicament of being human.

His account is an editorial and publishing puzzle: what is it? Psychology? Philosophy? Psychotherapy? Evolutionary biology? Spirituality? Theology? Self-help?… This very unusual book is all, yet none of these. Here, clearly, the whole is more than the sum of its parts.

Psychotherapy, my own life's work, vaunts the potential to enhance the life experience of most human beings and yet its benefits are often poorly explicated, then become largely misunderstood or ignored. Overlaps and confusions of territory and terminology are inevitable because psychotherapy, counselling, psychology and psychiatry are only partly divisible and distinct. And there is another level of abstraction: all the schools, models and theories – each bolstered by gurus and texts – can then further alienate the potential seeker from the healing powers of psychotherapeutic relationships. It is into this complicated mind-field of information and choice that David Zigmond brings a sharp focus to produce this masterpiece of a monograph that cuts through the academic and administrative jungle. The result is to entertainingly engage and inform the interested reader about their own development and the potential for acceptance or change.

The author has been working with people for half a century, using and refining his own intuitive insight into the human condition through his role as GP, psychiatrist and psychotherapist. For almost forty of those years, he and I have been meeting and discussing many aspects of healing, therapy, relationships, and services for patients … amidst all of life's vicissitudes. Inevitably, given the span of years, we witnessed a multitude of changes and fashions in psychotherapy-packaging, service provision and access routes for therapeutic help in our Welfare services. At the heart of all these discussions, in both of our working lives, has been the desire to create conditions under which we fellow humans – in all our variety and heterodoxy – can enhance our quality of life, face and manage our difficulties, and then better fulfil our potential. For both of us, this lifelong mission has brought many rewards in witnessing the relief of suffering, yet quite as many disappointments as we witnessed services being decimated, and then dominated by regimes of managerialism and markets that lose their understanding and attunement for the individual. This is the background from which this magnificent small book is written. In its brevity, it playfully and pithily re-views our thoughts, feelings and behaviours in a way that will demystify psychotherapy and so make it accessible to all who are curious enough to understand. David Zigmond's chance invitation to Antwerp to talk about psychotherapy to Jain Indian diamond dealers provided an eccentric opportunity to refine and condense his ideas and so capture something of the essence of the human condition, and then the potential routes for understanding and change. His dialogue of questions and answers leads us to straightforward explanations of phenomena that are refreshingly clear and free from the use of jargon.

Much confusion arises from our many psychotherapy tribes. There is much antagonism between them, each claiming to convey The Truth and to have The Answers. Some tribes are bolstered by highly influential statistical research evidence that gives them leverage over other models that do not: there is here a blind disregard for the fact that more holistic, relationship-based therapies are not so easily reduced to measurable behavioural outcomes. This easily skews our understanding and evaluation, and then misleads us. We are reminded here that one size does not fit all; the uniqueness of each individual is often paramount. If we are not careful, we can be dazzled by science and then not see ways of thinking that science cannot register or capture.

*

As soon as I read this book, many things fell into place for me, rather belatedly in my career. Despite reading hundreds of books on human development and therapeutic theories and treatments, I had often missed the elemental questions: Why do we suffer? And how do we heal? reflected in this book's sub-title. The uniqueness of this writing is how its rich breadth is expressed with such serious but humorous clarity. David Zigmond starts his straightforward definition and depiction of the challenges that life poses for us all: facing mortality, being alone, finding reassurance in relationships, and meaning in our lives. He goes on to show how the inevitable anxieties generated by living in the future or the past, rather than the present, create much of our distressed confusion. Psychotherapists pay much attention to the attempts we make to manage these anxieties: displacement, denial, projection and other problematic defences – these are clearly illustrated and explained here. His discussion of the healing elements of so many of our 'ordinary' relationships leads seamlessly into the need for 'therapeutic relationships' – those that are specifically created and pursued to help us achieve better responses and equilibrium everywhere else. The account of how dis-ease may sometimes lead to disease vividly maps out some fascinating and important territory.

The analogy made with the uncontrived experience and love that a dog provides its owner seems magically consummate to me as a dog lover. Dogs live in the present, harbour no grudges and are immediately grateful for all the indulgences offered to them. If only human relationships could be so simple and rewarding! It is links such as these that make *Humanity's Conundrum* so accessible, even to psychotherapy-phobics or the utterly uninformed.

As for God and his experiment – in first creating the world, and then human beings with just a bit too much brain and imaginative capacity – both *Genesis Revisited* and the Divine Creator may be questionable, but the result is surely plain for all to see. We tie ourselves up in knots while trying to train and restrain our instincts and desires. Thank goodness that writers like David Zigmond are putting their extra brain power to such good use in writing a book that provides such a valuable framework for understanding ourselves, and then offers us an optimistic view as to how we humans can help, instead of obstruct or torment, ourselves and others.

That, surely, is worth our time and attention.

Emeritus Professor Sue Wheeler

University of Leicester

February 2021

Prologue:
An accidental conception?

This book had some unusual and unlikely beginnings.

In autumn 2018 I received a strange but attractive-sounding invitation: I was asked to go to Antwerp to introduce an interested group of resident Jain Indians to the basic ideas of psychotherapy. Almost incomprehensibly they were neither associated professionals nor trainees; mostly the participants worked in the completely unrelated and ancient Antwerp diamond trade. So why the invitation? Well, the interest of the Jain Indians had been stoked by one of their members, J, who had been the first among them to do any kind of psychotherapy training in the UK. She, the trainee-pioneer, wanted an outsider to the clan to come and explain this apparently arcane world to them.

J's request was initially for a day seminar on 'Psychodynamic Psychotherapy', but I thought this too technical and earnest in tone, and too limited in scope to match what I hoped would be their untried yet likely curiosity. I wanted something looser and more wide-ranging. Rather than talk about the conventions of packaging of psychotherapy, I would rather address the fundamental human questions behind why such an activity should exist at all. *Why do we suffer? And how do we heal?* seemed a good place to start.

Soon after this invitation I went to a lecture by a neuropsychologist, who described how wondrously adaptive is our human brain-functioning to our biological and social lives; what a triumph of teleology we have to depend on! The audience seemed to agree but I had, and have, many misgivings. If our brain is so adaptive, why do we make our environment and many of our relationships so unviable? Why can we not stop doing things? Why do we so often crave the unhealthy, the painful or even the (self) destructive? In short, why are humans so anguished and conflicted, so restive and restless?

No, I thought, the human brain is not adaptive, it is uniquely maladaptive in its sophistication. How and why has this happened? Well, in the end, there is always a point where we cannot answer such basic questions, so then we invent myths and fables. The Bible does this with the origin of Life and seemed good enough in accounting for the world's many species and ecosystems for many centuries before our scientific enlightenment. But I don't think it ever did well with its account of human anomalies. So, for this 21st century, the relevant bits need a re-write: hence *Genesis Revisited*, my opening chapter. This biblical revision accounts, I think, rather better for the perverse anomalies that make Homo sapiens such a distinct species. In this way the redacted Biblical myth may work well as both explanation and prediction: our history and our future.

This parodic play on orthodoxy worked extremely well in the Antwerp seminar: the participants rapidly overcame their initial puzzled and polite deference and reticence to become lively and engaged discussants. (All this was helped by their excellent command of English.) I have since extended this narrative to other ideas of why we suffer and how we heal, hence *An alternative psychology.*

The following monograph is derived from piecemeal and reconstituted transcripts from the Antwerp gathering and, since then, from seminars with psychotherapy and medical trainees. The dialogue is thus all real but necessarily edited, and sometimes reordered, for clarity and brevity. Participants' questions or brief comments are designated by 'D', for discussant.

This wide-spanned, broad brush-stroked portrayal of our human condition is written more for general readability than specialist or academic convention. Science is drawn on to fuel bold speculation but not exhaustive or exacting scholarship. In this spirit, numerous references or academic footnotes have been avoided: instead I have settled for an explanatory Appendix.

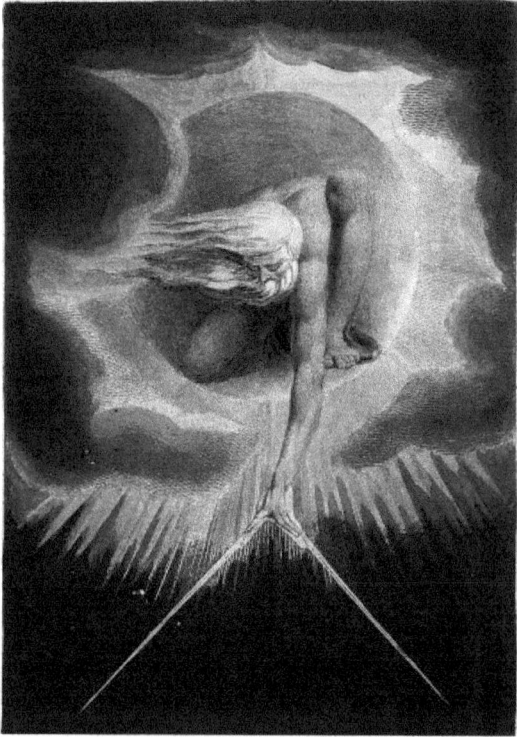

The Ancient of Days, William Blake 1794

Chapter One:

Genesis Revisited: In the beginning

All things bright and beautiful
All creatures great and small
All things wise and wonderful
The Lord God made them All

Well, of course we all know the story of our very beginning: in brief, God created the world in six days, saw that it was Good and so He rested on the seventh day – the first-ever sabbatical.

This official account – *Genesis* – tells us that everything was hunky-dory until Adam and Eve spoiled God's order(s) by eating the apple of temptation, thus blaming mankind forever for its tragic predicaments.

Well, modern research from neuroscience and evolutionary biology indicates that there was probably an ancient cover-up here, and that the story of the apple was a decoy. This cover-up, it is now alleged, goes right to the top, and it is surely notable that He avoids all pleas for direct interviews and thus any comment…

The latest research amounts to this: God did create the world in six days and it was good. In fact, it was probably too good, because it seems that after resting for a few hours on the seventh day He looked very closely at His very complex creation. He could quickly see it was perfect – the innumerable life forms were seamlessly enmeshed and balanced and would be sustainable for an eternity.

Yet this perfection brought Him not pleasure, but consternation: for divine beings much prefer eternally awesome projects to mere fixing, monitoring, maintenance or tinkering. The outlook of such semi-retirement for the next thousand million years or so was not fit for any God.

So, He set himself a puzzle and a challenge. What would happen if He endowed just one of the species with a much larger brain than was needed for social and individual survival – the need of all creatures for food, shelter and procreational encounters? If He granted only to this one species merely a fraction of His own illimitable intelligence, what would happen?

*

Well, right from the start, this divine experiment, in providing a surfeit of brain capacity, ran into problems that were very interesting – even unique – amongst living things. And those problems multiplied.

To begin with, because of the size of the brain, the baby had to spend much time in the mother's body before birth to protect its very early, fragile development. That long period, together with the developing large head, placed great strains on the mother's body – even more so if she carried more than one simultaneously.

The mother and baby then both faced greater difficulty – peril even – at the time of birth as the passage of the large head out of the mother was mechanically difficult, sometimes impossible. So, until very recently birth was often accompanied by death or serious damage to the mother, baby or both. This was much less common amongst other creatures and haunted the highly conscious, large-brained humans: birth and death were often forced to come together, and with unprecedented consciousness. This consciousness – of intertwined opposites, of ineradicable paradoxes – then drove humans' ceaseless attempts to deny or resolve its contradictions. As we shall see, these efforts, over aeons of time, were rarely successful: they become uniquely human.

*

Nor did things get rapidly easier for this vulnerable couple after birth, because the baby's body and brain still needed much more time to develop: it was born very helpless and with few autonomous abilities. This was very different to most mammals, whose newborn were often running around and frolicking within a few days, sometimes hours.

This human baby, waiting for its very large brain to develop, would be very vulnerable and dependent for many years. And this needed a stable, surrounding network of long-term relationships with and between adults to provide the extensive necessary protection, nurturance and guidance. Such caretaking thus made great demands on the caretakers – the adults with fully-grown brains – and the long bonds of dependency.

Such protracted and complex dependencies – like very intricate mechanisms – were subject to breakages and failures of the component parts or their linkages. This led not only to temporary setbacks of development but also to more lasting and propagating malfunctions. This was because the large brain capacities did not just remember parental failures, but also elaborated on them: first elaborated on these failures individually, and then passed these elaborations on to others – often to the next generation. All these are features of humans' unstoppable imagination – the speculative realm of what is not-there. This, indeed, was an early indication of a particularly human tendency – the urge to keep doing or imagining things even when these cannot address current realities and are not helpful. More on this later.

So, even before these excessively-brained creatures reached their maturity they were already likely to accrue many difficulties; this was true both of the dependent juveniles and their many necessary caretakers. The experiment was certainly interesting to the Divine Designer: what would happen next?

Chapter Two:

Exosphere*: What humans did next

The layer of atmosphere furthest from the earth

Man is the only animal for whom his own existence is a problem which he has to solve and from which he cannot escape.

– Erich Fromm, *Man for Himself*. 1947

Well what the experiment showed was that the long gestation of the human – from embryo to adult – created great difficulties far beyond biological maturation. For these large-brained creatures not only amplified and elaborated the almost inevitable failures of their prolonged dependency, (yes, we all have some) but, having made it to adulthood, humans often struggled to then find positive use for their large brain capacity. Once they had acquired shelter, food and procreational access, what would they do? Other creatures would then, mostly, settle contentedly with such equilibrium, maybe indulging in periodic play or grooming, but mostly satisfied with what is there. But not humans: instead they showed a pattern of inexhaustible interest in what is *not there,* often very much at the expense of what is – 'current reality'. So it was that humans became seduced, sometimes inspired, quite as often tormented, by what was not there – what their imaginations created.

D: Can you say more about this 'what is not there'?

Yes. Humans' capacity for this is crucial to understanding both the comparative brilliance and the tragic and destructive foolishness that distinguishes them. Let's continue with the story as it will make this clearer…

So, the human adult, having been shepherded and protected for this long period from the time of his often hazardous birth, is now 'free' to make use of this great surfeit of thinking capacity. What then happens to this burgeoning? Well, some of this is channelled into inventiveness to assure evolutionary advantage: to gain speed, mechanical power, more defensive structures, predictable food supplies, for example. But the human brain is rarely satisfied by such securements: as far as we can tell, more than any other animal, our behaviour is more and more determined by what is not there than what is, and that these 'not theres' become more and more abstract.

D: What does that mean?

It means that the human doesn't just ask questions like: I wonder if there are better fruit over the hill, in the next valley? Or, if I climb up to, shelter in, that cave will I be warmer and safer? All higher primates, too, seem constantly to be considering such 'not theres'.

But the human capacity and appetite for increasing abstraction far exceeds this. We, more and more, think of fictitious worlds that have often decisive influence over how we then behave. What is death? Can I avoid it? What happens to 'me' when I am no longer here? If other humans do not acknowledge me, do I really exist? Can I make other people think like me? Am I condemned to, and by, my separate consciousness and its unbidden thoughts? Can I ever rid myself of all this? Is there a Divine Being who can answer these questions that so trouble me? Can I commune with this Divine Being? If not me, is there some other human that can? And how would I recognise them? And eventually, the primal question: what is the meaning of my life? And that of others?

D: Is this really so important?

Oh, yes! I do believe so. Consider this: humans are the only species, as far as I know, that will deliberately kill itself. That comes from not being able to answer such questions, yet not being able to stop them either. And it is worse still: I think that is, often, why humans kill other humans, too…

D: But why? Where do these questions come from?

It seems to me that humans, because of their excess brain capacity, have become haunted and harried by a consciousness that far exceeds its functional requirements. This has precipitated four near-universal, certainly perennial, basic 'existential anxieties'…

D: What is that, these 'existential anxieties'*?*

Well, as the term suggests, these are anxieties seemingly inseparable from human existence. So they are the troubling doubts and fears that we are liable to have throughout, and because of, our lives. They seem to be the ineradicable price we pay for our cerebral surplus and its overspilling consciousness. The anxieties thus both cause, and seem to have become rooted in, human nature and its existence – hence its name, 'existential anxiety'. Angst, I think, is another word that captures something similar…

D: Yes, but what are they?

Well, that brings us to the next chapter.

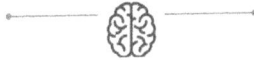

The Scream, Edvard Munch 1910

Chapter Three:

The Four Existential Anxieties:
Why we suffer

It seems to me that humankind has had to contend, for as long as speech has existed, with four basic existential anxieties. Because of their power to generate fear and dread we often try not to think about them, so then they become 'unconscious': but this doesn't make them less influential, it sometimes makes them more so because we are then more at the mercy of unperceived influences...

D: Yes, but again, what are they?

OK, here they are. I'll list them with some brief comments:

1. Death. All humans, from prepuberty onwards, have awareness, then knowledge, of the inevitability of their death.

There is some evidence that elephants have some such recognition, but mostly humans seem markedly alone with this realisation.

A few hundred years ago, in France, La Rochefoucauld wrote: 'Neither the sun nor death can be looked at steadily.' This captures well, I think, the ever-present fear and fascination that come with such knowledge.

And, of course, we have devised many ways of denial, consoling ourselves or – worst of all – attempting to put our fear or final destiny into other people.

More of all this later.

2. *Aloneness.* We are often aware of the singularity of our own consciousness; sometimes this is intolerable for us.

Margaret Mead, an anthropologist, many decades ago advised a student: 'Always remember that you are absolutely unique, just like everyone else!' This is paradoxical and witty and captures an important truth – that our alone-consciousness is what we share in our humanity. We build bridges to others, throughout our lives, of extraordinary variety and ingenuity. We do this to mitigate and reduce that aloneness: to bear being *apart*, we must find ways of being *a part*.

3. *Insignificance.* Humans, by perceiving the much vaster space and time than they inhabit, then understand their cosmic insignificance.

This life-and-time-beyond-themselves is very much a human imagination and perception-capacity, and is compounded, often painfully, by our simultaneous sense of mortality – in the larger picture we can readily see how our tiny significance rapidly disappears with our individual life. Our technology – satellites and telescopes, for example – tell us very precisely how illimitably vast is everything that is not-us, thus how cosmically insignificant we all are… And, then, even worse, we know we are all going to die!

How do we bear this? Well, we must find ways of seeking, inventing and conferring significance with others. 'You will be significant for me, if I can be significant to you': this psychology and signalling accounts for most of human social behaviour.

4. Meaninglessness. Nothing inherently has any meaning; meaning is something we must invent and generate. Life seems intolerable – unsustainable even   without meaning.

So humans are meaning-seekers, yet meaning is elusive to our most powerful and reliable intellectual tool: our science. Science may define mechanism, but never meaning. This confronts us with a painful deficit and vulnerability: we must inhabit a meaningless world inscrutably indifferent to our fears and yearnings.

Where to turn? Science has no answers. Philosophy can only offer us more questions. Religious and political ideologies will give us (or force on us) other people's 'definite' answers. 'I must find a system or live by another man's,' wrote the poet and artist William Blake. That is a harsh dilemma.

The dangers here are obvious, yet many choose the easier submission rather than face a meaning-vacuum.

What then? Many twentieth century writers have thought that this is mankind's most important and tricky problem: how each of us must find meaning in our lives, either with or without other people.

D: How are all these existential anxieties related to the too-much-brain and 'not-theres' you have been talking about?

Well, these anxieties are what, in some form, the human mind produces, and then has to contend with, once our elemental, 'animal' needs – for food, shelter, procreation – are met. They seem an inevitable product of our cerebral excess – what the brain turns to once irreducible, more biological, needs are satisfied.

And, yes, these anxieties are related to, and created by, our imagination – for imagination is essentially conjuring what is not there. And so it is that our imagination then haunts us with spectred vanishings of what we most value: of meaning, of connection, of significance, or of life itself – these imagined losses spawn our four basic anxieties.

D: Isn't this true also of some other animals?

Occasionally maybe, but only slightly. Mostly not. For example, primates often seek social inclusion and status within their group. They may show signs of dispiritedness if they do not have this. Of course, this is also true of humans; but humans can have status and inclusion and still go on to kill themselves. As far as I know, that has no animal-equivalent: the decisively human factor here is the wider meaning that is so insistently sought or conferred, and becomes so intolerable in its absence.

D: So do you see this as the root of human suffering?

In many ways, yes. Although I would emphasise the word 'human' because there are other forms of suffering that we share, I think, with many other creatures: pain, hunger and, in some higher mammals probably, grief. I would call this kind of suffering 'biological', as distinct from the kinds of suffering that come, specifically, from our human cerebral excess – our existential anxieties; our torment from imagined not-theres.

D: Why is that distinction important?

Well, biological suffering is relieved by simple kindness and specific physical remedies – food, shelter, warmth etc. Human existential suffering requires a different and more complicated kind of understanding and approach…

D: Is that psychotherapy?

Only sometimes. Wait and see!

Vampire II, Edvard Munch 1895

Chapter Four:

Who will suffer, and how?

So this view of this kind of human suffering sees it as some variety of failing to contain or counter any of our existential anxieties. This means that anything that inflames and intensifies these anxieties will sicken us and…

D: Do you mean makes us actually ill?

Yes, certainly sometimes…

D: What? Physical and mental illness?

Yes, sometimes either, sometimes both. The more diseased and distressed we are from our existential anxieties, the more likely we are to become disabled by some form of illness. There's a lot of research showing statistically how all kinds of illnesses are related to self-perceptions of aloneness, insignificance and loss of meaning. That's been found to be true across the whole span of illnesses, from the trivial to the fatal.

D: So our experiences, and how we interpret these, can make us sick?

Yes. If it is not our experiences, then it is our imaginations: 'nature abhors a vacuum' and, as we have seen, our cerebral excess will often fill any vacuum – any empty space – with existential anxieties: the morbid 'not-theres'.

So another way of expressing this is to say that our existential anxieties are 'vacuum phenomena': how our excessive brains default to fill the gaps with our dreads, our morbid imaginings…

D: So we – we humans – have a lifelong task: to avoid the gaps and see off our existential anxieties.

You got it! Yes, it's a lifelong task both for ourselves, and with and for one another. Positively engaged, it accounts for most of our tolerable, or even inspiring, social behaviour. But when massively denied, it leads to the horrors we may inflict on one another.

D: I've lost you. What does that mean?

Well, in our attempt to escape the awareness of our aloneness, our cosmic insignificance, our meaninglessness and our mortality, we may wish to inflict and control these conditions on, and with, others: we force on them what we most fear. This projection onto others has the intention or illusion of immunity: 'you *are the one who will be insignificant, alone and must have a meaningless death, not me!*' Hence many of our (often rationalised) hatreds and intolerances. At its most massive and grotesque it leads first to murder, then to genocide and death camps.

Similarly, our compulsive need – sometimes obsession – to have access to and into others' bodies can often be understood as an attempt to ablate the pain of singularity.

D. 'Access to and into others' bodies', *you say … is that sexual relationships?*

Yes, but certainly not always.

D: What's the distinction, then?

Well, generally social contact is with our outside body – our clothes and our skin (ectoderm); sexual contact enters our inner body's membranes (endoderm). Sex is then our exchanges at the junction of our inner and outer bodily selves. Our dis-ease here is common, may be universal, especially with our sexual appetites. Serious transgression and destruction obviously represent the more desperate and disturbing attempts to assuage our unbearable singularity, our sense of apart-ness.

D: But sex isn't the only way we resort to such awful measures, is it?

No, I agree. Our modern technology now shows us, with increasing frequency in the media, these kind of projections being acted out by mass stabbings, shootings or bombings by lone or clustered, aggrieved assassins or 'martyrs'. What motivates such 'irrational' behaviour? Do they vainly hope for redemption by violently projecting into others their intolerable loss of meaning, significance and living connection? The frequent conflation of homicide with suicide seems to indicate such desperate thinking.

D: Ugh! I got that too, but don't want to stay there. Can we return to how we can help one another with all this?

Sure, but that last and very uncomfortable notion is worth lingering over. For it shows the terrible price we can pay for not being able to face and handle our existential anxieties. Such abuse, or just oblivious disregard, we can term 'pathogenic': a medical term for that which breaks down our health. Here we are talking about the profound social and personal disrespects that make us dis-eased or ill.

So, back to your request: how do we help, or even heal?

Let's go there now.

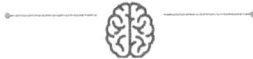

Tobias Healing His Father's Blindness, Rembrandt 1640

Chapter Five:

How do we heal?

So how do we best heal, either ourselves or others? How do we offer comfort, contain damage, and then enable our capacities for immunity, growth and repair to become determinant?

We've talked about the peculiarly human forms of suffering that arise from our surfeit of memory and imagination. Knowledge of these can then guide how we may best comfort and heal. These – comfort and healing – need this guidance because their interactions are nuanced and complex: any of their effectiveness is due to the human (experiential) rather than the technological (manipulative)…

D: Too complicated and too many long words already! I'm lost. What do you mean?

Oh, sorry, too fast… OK, simpler language. Here's another approach, too. Let's consider the difference between treatment and healing.

Treatment and healing are very different, though we sometimes do them together. Treatment is more 'doing to' a person and usually depends on impersonal technology; healing (which is an extension of comfort) is about 'being with' a person and depends on the quality of personal contact and understanding, and how that is experienced – in short, a relationship.

D: So treatment is more about impersonal science, and healing is about... what? Humanity?

Yes. Humanity, empathy, art, imagination... that sort of thing. So, to distinguish: treatment is about objective technical knowledge and needs some kind of a specialist to administer it; healing is rather about personal understanding and doesn't depend on that kind of specialist knowledge...

D: What does it need then?

The different kind of skills of personal understanding and attunement. And those necessarily involve imagination and intuition: for example, accurately 'guessing' what the person has not said, after carefully listening to what was actually said. So these are more complex and subtle – often personally encoded – forms of human encounter. And that means we cannot readily manage or determine such engagements by procedures, rules or measurements. I hope you can see that, unlike treatment, healing must involve some kind of personal meaning and relationship... that's crucial...

D: What about self-healing? Isn't that also important?

Indeed it is. Well, even here we need a good relationship with ourselves: people who have lost a sense of self, or purpose, or belonging are far more likely to get ill and then fail to heal. Most of us know this from experience, and research has shown it many times.

D: So how is all this related to our existential anxieties?

I'll put it like this: anything that contains, counters or quietens any of our existential anxieties is first comforting and then, possibly, healing. I would also say that any such comfort or healing interaction is 'psychotherapeutic' – that's not necessarily the same as 'psychotherapy': this is an interesting and important distinction which we'll return to later.

What this means is that any utterance, act or presence that adds to our sense of personal significance, human resonance or greater meaning will comfort and help heal.

D: I notice you haven't there mentioned the D-word...

Ah. Death! Well, you're right. Death is the one haunting that is least easily countered. Yet even that haunting becomes much less if we carefully tend our other three anxieties: if we find significance with others, find positive ways of communing with their consciousness, and then make sense and purpose in this bigger-than-me world – then death's inevitability usually loses its terror... Incidentally I think this philosophy makes the larger human part of our best terminal care...

D: What happens if it doesn't?

Well, even in this 21st Century we still have the option of various religions that can offer you an attractive afterlife, though that is usually dependent on strict faith-compliance. In medieval times it was rather better: by merely purchasing an Indulgence from the Catholic Church they would reserve you a place in heaven – no previous compliance was necessary, just payment. So, our assumption that modernity always brings us more convenience is sometimes untrue…

D: More seriously though, is your understanding of healing – the answers we find to these main anxieties – something we can all do, throughout our lives?

Oh, yes! That's a very important point. How each person deals with these universal basic anxieties tells us much about what kind of life they are likely to have. How we counter, or submit to, or flee from these things – the knowledge of our mortality, our alone-consciousness, our wider insignificance, our void of ultimate sense – will largely determine the quality and nature – and often the story – of our particular life. It is likely, too, to play a large part in our mental health and important aspects of our physical health…

D: But, surely, these personal attitudes and spiritual strengths – because I think that's what you're talking about – can't change things like genetics, can they?

In many ways you're right. There are many things in our fate that are beyond our control, like your example of genetics. Yet what often proves decisive about how these *forces majeure* play out, and our experience of them, is how we deal with our primal and ineradicable life-anxieties. How do each of us carry or reject these burdens-of-consciousness?

D: So they're often the balancing factor…

Exactly. Yes, in the end we will all sicken and die, but between now and then, if we can find ways of creatively engaging our surplus brain activity – our existential questions – our lives become (mostly) healthier, less turbulent and probably longer.

D: So what is it we can do for one another?

Well, any such affirmative contact is likely to help the other's internal capacities for immunity, growth and repair – their experiences of comfort and healing…

D: Any such contact?

Yes. From a brief but friendly 'Hello', to an extended positive relationship of psychotherapy, both imply: 'you are significant for me, so not alone. We can make some kind of personal sense together to affirm and value our transient lives.' Of course, psychotherapy is a much more deliberate and intensive interaction. It is going to spend much more time developing and examining the preliminary sparks signified by any 'Hello', and also, equally important, how and why we may extinguish these… Many of our problems come from our irrational, sometimes unconscious, acts of extinction…

D: All this sounds a bit religious for me!

I think that's very understandable: many religions – at least in their origins, I think – are motivated to quell the anguish caused by the four existential anxieties. But religions then tend to provide answers from God, a unifying divinity; most psychotherapies provide a less impressive and clear-cut response – mere guidance for each of us to find our own, less perfect and complete, answers…

D: You said before that what is 'psychotherapeutic' is much wider than 'psychotherapy' – going to a specialist. I'm unclear what you meant.

Ah yes. I see this as a helpful distinction. I think that what is psychotherapeutic is any engagement or activity that boosts our internal resources. So that's an enormous proportion of our better human activity and relationships. But 'psychotherapy' – the specialist activity – is much more focused. It is the deliberate project of examining these questions and our responses to them, and then attempting to chart our best navigational course. And usually we do this with a designated person (the therapist) in a protected space (the consulting room).

D: Isn't that like going to a church or temple and being in the presence of the priest?

In many ways, yes. A church or temple is meant to be a special place where we can concentrate on bigger and higher purposes, and so transcend our basic anxieties about the lonely smallness and transience of our lives. And the priest is a kind of designated agent or officer to enable that. But we don't achieve these desired things just by going to the church or temple: something else is required to achieve this kind of transcendence. And this 'something else' comes in myriad ways: many can find this comfort, grace or peace in themselves, or in their important relationships, outside of any religious meeting or venue – they have what is 'psychotherapeutic' without any designated religion or consulting room...

D: So what's the place of psychotherapy? Who benefits from it?

Well, we can think of psychotherapy as a deliberately sought kind of skilled guidance and exploration. So it's only suitable for us if we want such guidance, are prepared to explore, and have an affinity for the particular approach and guide on offer.

D: Yes, but what sort of person will want that?

It can be anyone anguished – dis-eased – by their inability to make adequate human sense, connection, purpose or significance in their lives. So then – going back to our earlier discussion – we become increasingly in thrall to what is not there, rather than engaging with what is there.

D: What happens then? How do these things show?

What happens is akin to Archimedes' principle of displacement: the more mental energy that is engaged with what is *not* there, the less contact we can have with what *is* there. Our reception and perception of reality become displaced... we become lost in the labyrinth of abstractions and imaginations created by our singular large brains, and then cannot find a way out.

D: Does that always matter?

Not always, no. It depends on context, timing and quantity. For example, as long as we're safe we can go to sleep and dream, or stay awake and write a fictional story or musical composition – we can, by choice, allow submersion in the 'not-there' world, the realm of dream and our internal-world, our subjectivity … the overspill of our cerebral excess. These are harmless displacements; sometimes they rise to become the very positive source of valued creativity that is particularly human.

But at other times that 'not-there' world becomes preoccupied, flooded even, by our existential anxieties: we then get forms of mental dis-ease that are the embryonic forms – the precursors – of mental illness.

So let's take a closer look at what happens to our mental life when our excessive brain capacity generates too many not-theres.

The Great Red Dragon and the Beast From the Sea, William Blake 1805

Chapter Six:

Human dis-ease and its not-theres

We have seen how the biological human legacy of excessive brain capacity has generated our tendency to surplus memory and imagination – then how this leads to the hauntings of our four existential anxieties and our preoccupations with what is not-there, so often at the expense of what is.

Many conventional categories of mental dis-ease, and more serious mental illness can be understood in this way. Let us take an example and see how it works. We can then turn to some others.

Anxiety is a response to something that might or could be there but is (probably) not. It is a caught tangle from the mind's conjuring, not an adaptive behaviour to solve a real-life problem.

So our anxiety-states are not about actually being trapped in a lift, being bitten by a poisonous spider, being publicly humiliated, or our plane crashing. If these things really are happening, we most likely talk of the stark problem, rather than the expected emotional response. In contrast, anxiety is very much the offspring of our imagination.

Yet however maladaptive we deem our anxiety, it continues as a very common and highly distinctive human trait.

The truth of this is shown in how much of our social lives consists of devices and approaches to disperse or allay one another's anxieties. Indeed, *Homo anxietens* is probably a more accurate label than the more self-flattering *Homo sapiens*.

Such is our capacity – our compulsion – to be drawn to the not-there.

Depression is a term that has become so widely recruited to medical-type thinking that its human meaning risks getting lost. Nevertheless, in its commoner and milder forms it seems, like anxiety, to be a dis-ease of not-theres. So what's different? Well, while anxiety is a *fear* of what *might* be there, depression is *sadness* or *shame* for what *was* there, or *ought to be* there. Again, it is not about what is actually there. So, the depressed person says to themselves (and others): 'I *should* have/be/feel/do', 'I *was…*'. They may also project this onto the world, persistently lamenting its many not-theres.

If other animals dispirit themselves with their memory or imagination, it is much rarer. Animals confined and controlled by humans seem our commonest emulators: this probably says much about our contagious influence.

*D: You've described depression as being based on a lot of not-theres, but the awful feelings really **are** there and can be very serious. You don't dispute that, do you? And how do you account for it – something so real, based so often on what is not real?*

This is the power of the not-theres for we humans! Just by having *ideas* of how we or the world *could* be, or *should* be otherwise, we can easily create a restless unhappiness and dispiritedness that itself changes the way the brain works – first its physiology, then eventually its anatomy – and inevitably the body it signals to. So, yes, you're right: what we do with our existential ambiguities and vacuums has very real effects. And this is true throughout human life: our ideas and imaginations have much more effect on us, and the world around us, than merely asserting our mere biological existence and its needs. But let's now turn to a third category.

Psychosis is the most dominant, sometimes tyrannical, of the not-theres: our internal world of imagination does not just invite, or entice, or wheedle, or haunt, or nag – it *insists* and will hear of no alternatives.

So while anxiety fears what might be (but is not), and depression grieves for what is not, psychosis decrees that what is not, *is*. So while anxiety and depression may distort or impair our contact with reality, psychosis short-circuits this struggle by *replacing* external 'objective' reality with internal subjective reality. Not-there becomes Emperor: 'it is true because I think it'.

Other animals can, of course, misperceive or misconstrue but that is very different. Does any non-human creature so elaborate their not-theres as to persistently obliterate what is there? And if 'necessary', themselves?

Addictions, too, may be seen as a defence against, an avoidance of, our four existential anxieties. Humans obsessively pursue, then surrender to, a relationship, an activity or a chemical as a desperate attempt to escape from the overspilling brain's existential anxieties. The addict thus attempts to eclipse – or at least dull or displace – an otherwise intolerable sense of loneliness, insignificance and meaninglessness. And again the question: what other living form attempts to so disperse or destroy itself to escape its own imagination?

D: That word you use – dis-ease – sounds not too bad. But you're also talking about pretty serious things and they sound ill to me. How do you make the distinction?

A very important question. Let's consider that now.

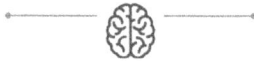

The Shipwreck, J. M. W. Turner 1805

Chapter Seven:

Dis-ease or disease? When does our anguish become illness?

'Dis-ease' sounds very similar to 'disease', yet that small separating hyphen usually conveys a large difference in meaning…

D: What is that difference, then?

Let's take each in turn.

When we talk of *dis-ease* we usually refer to an unwelcome feeling of tension, a disturbing loss of balance or equilibrium, a kind of hazy yet definite alarm signal. Sometimes this signalling comes more from our body, at other times we are more aware of it in arrested thoughts or tangled feelings. All these are disturbances of the *function* of the mind or body. Often we can recognise, too, that such dissonance reflects *us*; it is feeding back to us something significant about ourselves and our predicaments. As such, dis-ease signals an opportunity for self-knowledge for each individual, though we may sometimes, when perplexed or fearful, seek the guided support of others. Yet it remains our *individual* puzzle and predicament.

Disease, by contrast, tends to *structural* disruption of the body and thus its healthy functioning. Often disease has no meaningful signalling to the individual about other life predicaments. For example, someone with Congenital Heart Defects, Sickle Cell Anaemia or Retinal Detachment most likely experiences these substantial body changes as being very separate from the self. The disease here is an encumbering alien, not a signalling ally, as dis-ease so often is. And, being so separate from the self, disease then needs a separate person – a professional practitioner – for its understanding and relief.

D: But that's not always true, is it? Surely some real physical illnesses have messages for us…

Yes, this is often the case. Particularly, it is clearest, when that structural disease is consequent to stress, or lifestyle, or important life events.

D: Can you give some examples?

Oh, there are plenty: the most obvious and well-known are related to smoking, drinking, and diet. Then there's the more subtle ones: the breakdowns of health accompanying bereavement, family disruptions, moving home, children leaving, retirement and redundancy, and then – more apparently surprising ones – going on holiday, getting married, being promoted…

D: What sense do you make of all that? What do they have in common?

Well they all, in some way, reflect our existential anxieties – our struggle to keep at bay our sense of aloneness, insignificance, and the loss of personal meaning or predictable order.

D: But these abstract things don't always make us ill, do they?

No, but they can…

D: When? When and how can these things you're talking about – our dis-ease, our imaginations, our complex anxieties – make us actually ill?

OK. Let's go back to the beginning. We've considered how our human brain excess is particularly liable to be overwhelmed by its own activity. Often the individual's mind cannot cope with – cannot contain or navigate – its own overspilling imagination. Then we need to 'bale out' what we cannot assimilate. The not-copable-with becomes separated and split off as not-self: it becomes *illness*. And the more ill we are, the more help we need from the outside…

D: I still don't understand. Can you give some examples?

OK. Let's say you feel intimidated by your boss and her demands and feel a tightness in your chest, a dis-ease signal. You say to yourself: 'I feel oppressed by all this: what shall I do?' You are troubled but you are not ill.

But let's say instead you are incapable of managing this. Instead your self-agency short circuits to: 'Something terrible is happening: I can't think properly and I can't breathe. Somebody help me!' You may well be taken to the nearest A&E Department where, after many tests, you are diagnosed as having a Panic Disorder and despatched to a prescribed Care Pathway. You are now 'ill': who now has what responsibility?

There are medical texts written about Panic Attacks; none available about resentfully submissive employees!

*D: But that example is about a kind of mental health or life problem, although I can see that it's physically expressed. What about **real** physical illnesses?*

OK. Let's go back to our example and say, instead, that your dis-ease, your signal, instead settles to that of nauseous 'acid indigestion' when you swallow your anger with authority-figures. But you do not, or cannot, consider this in clear consciousness. So then you cannot change either your oppressive situation or your reaction of entrapped and humiliated frustration. Over time your stomach signals this by secreting more and more acid – a reaction of escalating functional dis-ease. As this continues, the excessive stomach acid first inflames, then destroys, then ulcerates the stomach lining; *functional dis-ease* has morphed into *structural disease*: a Duodenal Ulcer. In this transition, agency has passed from self to not-self. The Duodenal Ulcer is now regarded as an illness – a kind of hostile accretion to be nullified by an expert. This is a tricky trade-off: the self is relieved, but the body is endangered.

D: So, one of the things you seem to be saying is that humans get ill because of their large brains!

Yes, sometimes, but certainly not always. Clearly, all living creatures eventually ail and die. So there is biomechanical failure and fate before and beyond our excess brain predicaments. What is being focused on here is the particular stratum of human struggle and strain that lies on top of our biomechanical determinants and so often exacerbates those beneath. This – the peculiarly human problem of cerebral overspill – is what accounts for our hauntings by existential anxieties, our agitated preoccupations with not-theres, and our often lifelong, often desperate, compulsions to either find ourselves or lose ourselves.

D: And you see these as root causes of not only much of our struggles with mental health and dis-ease, but also with some real physical illness – disease – too.

Precisely. Though I'd stress it as a root cause, among others. Nevertheless, it's a massive problem, a fundamental design fault. Humans have known about it certainly since we started keeping records.

I blame the manufacturer.

The Wizard of Oz 1939

Chapter Eight:
So what is therapy for our psyches?

D: I want to get back to healing. What and where is psychotherapy in all this?

Well we have probably anticipated, already, many fragments of an answer: we can see that healing, together with comfort, must somehow tend and calm the existential anxieties of the other. That's not to say that this is a complete account or explanation of healing, but it does mean that this is a primary task: so that interactions that do this are mostly therapeutic, and that interactions that do not do this cannot be therapeutic.

D: I'm unclear about the word 'therapeutic'*: what do you mean?*

That's a very crucial thing to define and get clear. So it deserves a detailed answer… so sit tight!

I'm using the word 'therapeutic' here to mean any interaction that evokes in the other any or all of the following: an increased capacity not only to endure, but also to creatively encounter, complex and difficult life-problems; a reduction in disability or pain; an increase in positive engagements beyond the self; the arrest or reversal of physical disease processes; an overall improvement in a sense of equanimity and life-connection or, as Freud expressed it more pragmatically, our ability to live, love and work…

D: That is quite a list! Yet I think I can see the unifying principle, how they overlap. Does this apply to both physical and mental problems?

Yes.

D: What? Even with serious physical illnesses?

Yes, but maybe in a different way. For example, terminal care may powerfully address issues of aloneness, personal significance and meaning, but usually in subtle ways that are implicit in our manner and acts. Such comfort and healing may not delay the time of a death, but they will make dying a very different experience for the departed and their carers - we who are left behind.

That would contrast with a healing interaction with, say, a physically healthy person in long-term psychotherapy. There, the references to those anxieties would be talked about much more explicitly, and often explored at length.

But in all these forms of comfort and healing, certain experiences are crucial: a beneficent contact with other consciousness in a way that affirms our significance, a sense of meaning and kinship amidst the vastness beyond us… and that we are witnessed in making our own pattern and purpose.

D: This all sounds... kind of religious...

I can see that, and in a way I think it is. Although in 'lay-therapy' we do not invoke an external God or supernatural authority. But I think most religions have their elemental source in the same needs and dreads that motivate other kinds of therapeutic influence – to help one another quieten and contain our cerebral surplus: our restless fears and tendency to distressing entanglements with what is not-there...

D: But how does religion, by inventing mythical not-theres – help us deal more realistically with what is actually not there?!

Yes, what a tangle! It's both a paradox and an illusion. On one level, it's absurd. Yet these are keys to understanding ourselves; we humans often need to invent such vagaries to stay sane...

D: No, seriously...

I am being serious, and it's an important point. Often we need to believe, and have faith in, the mythical in order to cope with the real. So in order to bear our existential anxieties – our painful undertows of not-theres – we need to invent even bigger not-theres in order to displace them: Gods, gurus, immaculate conceptions, transcendent orgasms, idealised States, loves and ideologies, the value of gold... should we add the growth economy?... all are compensations for, or avoidances of, our deeper fears.

D: That all seems very far-fetched to me … I don't think most people would understand or accept it…

I think they do, albeit at an instinctive level.

D: What does that mean?

OK. Consider the film *The Wizard of Oz*, I believe the most popular film ever. I think that popularity is due to the way it reflects back to us, with exceptional charm and wit, our central life tasks: how to be better equipped to deal with those human questions that can so sicken us if we cannot find our personal inner resources…

D: I haven't seen that film for forty years! You'll have to remind me and explain some…

Well, we can't now recount the whole story, but the film's main themes and symbols are very relevant to our understanding here. Each major character represents a universal human task of personal development: the failure to address any of these leads to dis-ease or sickness. The Lion must find courage to be himself (Identity); the Tin Man his heart for others (Love); the Scarecrow his own thoughts (Logos); and Dorothy a place of peace, acceptance and kinship: 'finding my way home' (Belonging).

To re-own these, they must achieve something that seems impossible to them as individuals: destroy The Wicked Witch of the West – the despair, nihilism and hatred we can all harbour and inflict in our frustrated unhappiness.

So this Wicked Witch of the West can be understood as humankind's torment by, and then destructive attempts to eliminate, the four primary anxieties: our aloneness, our cosmic insignificance, senselessness and transience.

How do Dorothy and her compromised companions manage this fearsome task? They do so communally, pursuing a shared belief in a myth: the all-powerful Wizard of Oz. It is through faith in this mythical Other that they transcend their habitual (self-)limitation, subtly trance-formed, then transformed.

Dorothy later, accidentally, discovers that the Wizard is an unremarkable man operating a panoply of pyrotechnics to create such hypnotic charisma. Dorothy confronts him:

'You're a very bad man!', shouts Dorothy, through angry tears.

'No, I'm not a bad man. I'm a very good man. Just not a very good wizard…' comes a faltering, apologetic explanation.

The paradox here is that it was belief in a fictitious power beyond themselves (the Wizard) that enabled them to master the very basic fears in themselves. I think this principle accounts for much of our better religious and therapeutic influences.

D: Several times you've talked of 'therapeutic influence' *and* 'psychotherapy': *I'm still unclear about the distinction.*

Well I'm probably repeating myself somewhat, but here goes.

All our better contact with nature and other humans is likely to be psychotherapeutic which, roughly translated, means 'good for our mind' and thus, usually, our whole being. So that includes anything that strengthens our sense of connection, inclusion, purpose, agency, understanding... all the things that can counter our human-brained terrors of aloneness, insignificance and personal meaninglessness, culminating in our knowledge of inevitable death.

So you can see how innumerable human activities may be psychotherapeutic: they all depend on varieties and mixtures of humanity, intent and judgement. But this cuts both ways: our influences can be reversed to be destructive of these things. Our influences then cause sickness; they are 'pathogenic'. We can make ourselves and others ill. An analogy here is how we may either nourish or poison the roots of a growing plant.

Psychotherapy is a more deliberate project to understand, condense and refine such things. We consciously seek out another human – a therapist – who we believe, or hope, has the skills to guide us in the way we process these challenges and questions: how we individually perceive, construct and respond to our world. This is normally done, often in a regular and repeated pattern, in a private and quiet space to assure ambient peace and confidentiality...

D: Why would anyone want or need this secluded and concentrated psychotherapy if, as you suggested, more ordinary psychotherapeutic influences may already exist all around us?

A number of reasons.

The first is that we may need more than what we can readily find, or what is offered, in our quotidian life. We can draw an analogy here with the religious person who feels the need to go to a place of worship. While the worshipper may retain faith and spirit in their work-a-day lives, the temple or church offers both replenishment and anchorage by concentrating these to a more intensive level: the devotion and specialness become sustaining and fortifying. They may confer onto the priest, too, special powers that seem to reach realms otherwise unattainable. In reality, and in another context, the priest may – like the Wizard of Oz – admit to being and feeling much like his idealising congregants. So, again, while the role may depend on myth and fiction, the satisfactions and achievements it may bring can be very real…

D: So are you saying that psychotherapy – the professional activity – is all a wishful illusion; all faith but no reality?

Oh, no! Just because this is an essential ingredient of psychotherapy doesn't mean that's all there is to it. But your question brings us conveniently to another major reason for people to realistically pursue psychotherapy.

It is, again, because of human complexity – an inevitable consequence of our cerebral surplus. Not only may we have a lifetime of troubles from our not-theres and our existential anxieties, but often we cannot then adequately heal ourselves with life's ambient psychotherapeutic influences – in work, in love, in social and family relationships… sometimes these are not enough.

D: Why is that then? Why can't we just get on with what's out there?

Well, again, it's because our excessively active internal worlds displace our perception of the external world beyond our capacities for correction. So then we can't see what we're not seeing: how we may be overlooking, or denying, or destroying the 'natural' sources of support or nourishment – the 'psychotherapeutic influences' – that are readily there for us. We get lost, sinking into our own swampland: then we need a guide with a rope!

D: Can you give some examples?

Yes. Let us say our inner world in its imaginings generates many thoughts and feelings about people or situations that are not in the here-and-now: guilt, fear, shame, insecurity, anger, resentment, mistrust, anticipatory grief… Any one of these can tarnish or destroy very real opportunities to contentment and relationships. In this process we lose sight of how and why this is, and with this we lose our capacity for self-navigation and self-propulsion. If this isn't too bad, then a guide – a psychotherapist – may help.

But what if the problem is much worse than that? What if our brain is so autogenically inventive, and is so stuck and flooded with these excess thoughts and feelings, that we can no longer work, socialise or care for ourselves? What then? Then it is time for more than a guide: then we need a caretaker for our malfunctioning mind and welfare. That's more the world of management and medications: mental illness, psychiatry.

This is the severe and hazardous price we pay for the brain capacity that also blesses us with powers of invention and abstraction. The brain's surfeit that gets us to fly into outer space is also the one that cripples us in our inner space.

What other creature has such convoluted abilities, needs and afflictions?

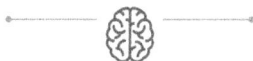

The Tower of Babel, Pieter Bruegel the Elder 1563

Chapter Nine:

How does psychotherapy work?

D: So how does psychotherapy work?

Ah! Another brief but difficult question. To answer it, we need to explain how may this arcane activity help us with our top-heaviness; the all-too-human self-made mazes and traps where we lose ourselves in our fictions and abstractions, our webs of not-theres?

The fact that so much is written about this, much of it in technical language, tells us just how complex are these human riddles. So in the space we have here, we can only draw out some of the core principles underlying how psychotherapists may help save us from and for ourselves…

D: Well, let's have some of those then!

OK, here are some ideas I've borrowed from basic physics about how things relate to one another and then change: the key words are 'conduction' and 'induction'. We'll see how these have their equivalents in attempting to help the anguished: 'conductive' and 'inductive' approaches. I can see here we need some definitions:

Let's take conductive approaches first. These emphasise a conveyance of *external* (to the person) agents or instructions to bring about relief. This is clearly the basis of medical 'treatments' where *external* agents (chemicals, needles, sutures, implants, radiations etc) are conducted to, and into, the patient. There are kindred forms of psychotherapy (mostly technically designated 'cognitive' or 'behaviour') that attempt, similarly, to directly change a person's experience or behaviour by externally conducting the therapist's structured programme – specific questions or instructions – to the obedient patient: any improvement is then thought to be due to the therapist's expert resources of specialist knowledge and manipulations, much like that of a surgeon's operation. These conductive therapies, or 'psychological treatments', are not the sort we will be exploring here.

D: Why not?

Well, the conductive approaches are more directly manipulative and mechanical and so are not based on considerations of imagination and choice – the basis of our exploration here. So let's now return to induction.

Inductive therapies, by contrast, evoke or activate or strengthen a person's own *internal* resources, the capacities they already have, even if they have lost touch with them. These are the approaches we are considering here.

D: I'm getting a bit lost. I've never been clear about what 'induction' *means...*

OK. Let's return to our basic science.

The word 'induction' has an interesting use in physics. A hundred and fifty years ago, seminal discoveries were made showing how the passage of a copper wire across a magnetic field produced a new phenomenon: an electric current which came into being only when the one object moved close to the other. The current is thus relational and conditional to the two objects: it does not occur in either alone, or when they are at rest, or distant.

Much of this applies to the inductive therapies and can explain them: the relationship between the sufferer and the therapist (or group) and the working context are essential to awakening and generating a kind of 'human current'. We can't really measure this current directly, but we can see its effect. It is this human current that brings about our influences of comfort, healing and growth – the elements and inductions of psychotherapy.

D: What's the difference between those – comfort, healing and growth?

Well they, first, must all involve a kind of 'tuned-in' accompaniment: we need to have good and accurate engagement – empathy. If that is achieved, then comfort may help us endure pain; healing restores our functioning; and growth enables still further possibilities.

D: And is all this related to the 'not-theres' *and the basic anxieties you keep referring to?*

Yes. The establishment of these positive human currents all help us deal with our complex fashionings of our fears, our dispiritedness, our rage, our blame, our shame… for all the ways we and the world are bound to fail one another, and what we then fear of our fate...

D: I read somewhere that we're all scared, and we all want some form of love.

I think that's a pithy and alternative way of expressing much of this. Of course, the way we express, or deny, or displace that fear varies massively and is often heavily disguised. The therapist's skill is to supportively decode, motivate and navigate. All of that is true, too, of our need for love. In fact, one good-as-any definition of adult human love is that it is a crucial relationship that helps us bear – sometimes transform – our existential anxieties: aloneness, insignificance, meaninglessness and death. The converse of that, of course, is that the breakage or withdrawal of that love can rapidly heighten those anxieties beyond our capacity to tolerate or contain them...

*D: What about love of animals? I **really** love my dog. I really love him!*

Yes, indeed! Animals have much to teach us, although I am unsure if that is their intent. I think we can often feel more at peace among other animals because they do not amplify or echo our existential anxieties, as other humans often do. Between humans, those anxieties often become exacerbated or contagious.

D: What do you mean?

Well, think of all the ways we have of distancing or even quarantining other people with excessive, and then infectious, fear or despair.

But let's get back to our safer canines. I imagine that loving your dog is so easy because he lives almost entirely in the present: his memory and anticipation seem very brief. His avoidances or urges may be idiosyncratic but rarely ruinous to himself or his environment. Does he ever harbour a grudge against you, or feign pleasure, to mask his fantasised contact with other dog owners?

D: I don't think so. Once, when I was doubtful about myself, I did ask him, but he ignored my question…

Exactly. Quite right too! He probably understands your question perfectly well but thinks it's utterly unimportant! That's because, beyond his biological needs, he is only interested in immediate and achievable pleasures in the *here* and *now*. He's not trying to reconfigure the past or engineer the future…

So when you're with your dog, he helps you to be a bit more like him: to live in the present, alive to its transient pleasures… and not concerned – at least for a while – with our entangling and leeching not-theres.

D: So dogs can be therapeutic?

Yes, definitely. But only if we enter into their mental world a little and allow them to teach us… For that we have to find our own kindness and patience.

There's a fascinating and amusing paradox here. Many religious and meditative practices urge us to an enlightened Higher Self, a state divested of yearnings, hauntings and expectations – a world now unencumbered by not-theres. Freed from these intrusions, we can then receive the here-and-now in a purer state: many describe this as transcendent, often using mystical or religious language. At such times we float free from our existential anxieties. The paradox is that humans need all this arcane language, thought and ritual to get back to the simplicity of being with, then being like, your dog… being part of nature…

D: So why have a therapist if you can have a dog?

Well, a therapist can help you see and understand all the internal ways you have of stymying contact with your inner-dog: all the ensnarements you have in echoing memories and fantasised fears, the hidden store-rooms you have, all jumbled with such hindrances. We need self-knowledge to be able to map, and then navigate, these kinds of inner obstructions and destructions. But this is not just confusing, it is often daunting, even frightening: that's why we then need a skilled guide.

A dog cannot do that, though its spirit may certainly encourage us.

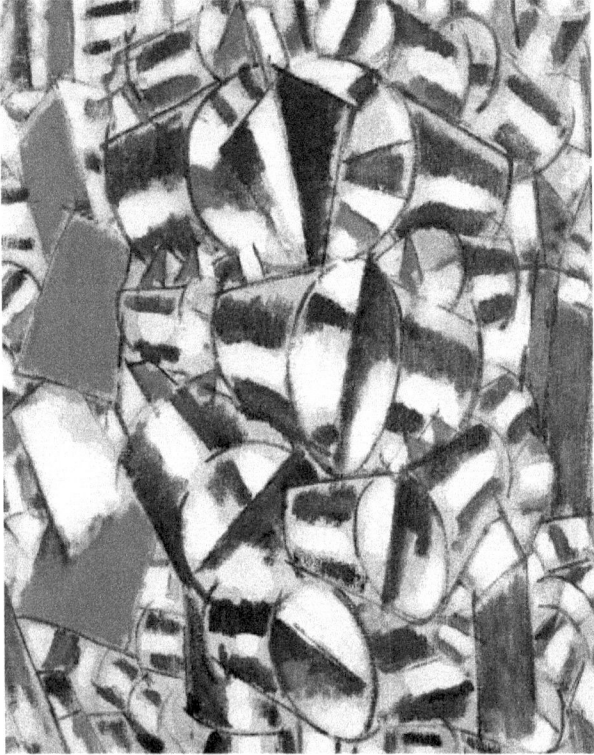

Contrast of Form, Fernand Leger 1913

Chapter Ten:

Why are there so many different kinds of psychotherapy?

*D: I think I'm now understanding much about the spirit and
intent of all this. But what I don't understand is why are there
so many different kinds of therapy? There seem to be more
and more!*

Indeed, that's correct. Maybe it's similar to the evolution
of fissioning religions. There, the originating motivations
and missions are often thought to have common roots, yet
they, too, then usually fragment, to emphasise particular
aspects or perspectives. Any one of these can then be
separated, branded and then pushed along its own
trajectory to develop its own maxims, myths and
language. The history of the major religions shows, too,
how each faction often attempts to exclude or destroy
other perspectives… in order to claim greater 'certainty' in
the mastery of not-theres!

In religion that division leads to cults and sects, each with
its own hierarchy, rituals and articles of faith. Similar
things have happened in psychotherapy. Then we have the
addition of a modern-times inevitability: commodification
and marketisation.

*D: Can you say anything more to help understand what all
these different kinds of therapy are?*

Well I think it's helpful to first think about how we all – us humans - operate. Basically we can conceive of our experience and expression in both mental and physical terms – thoughts/feelings and body/behaviour respectively. These can be thought of as primary elements, aspects or dimensions of experience, as in Figure 1, below.

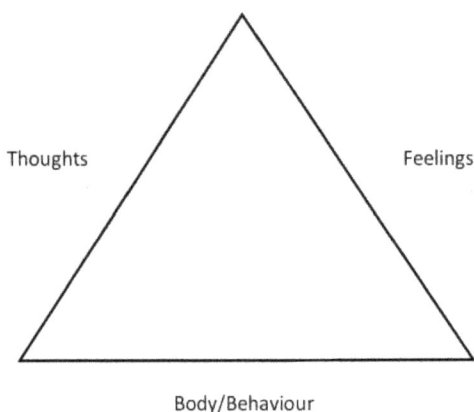

Figure 1: Personal experience, expression and portals of entry

All of us have all of these, of course. Yet individually and culturally, we may have an easiest or primary mode: this is our 'favourite' or default 'valency' – the conscious portal and base through which we receive, transmit and experience ourselves and the world. It is where we are most comfortable, spend most of our conscious time, and develop our most fluent language. Often we relegate other aspects to relative oblivion or unconsciousness: there are many people who are only comfortable – conscious even – through their thoughts, or their feelings, or their body, or what they are doing.

So each proclivity is manifest both in our individual consciousness (our inner world), and how we most readily seek out and then interact with others (our social world): each domain has its own language and style of discourse.

D: How is that related to all these different psychotherapies then?

Well, what happens is that ways of attempting to understand and alleviate anguish parallel this and can thus be designated in the same way. We have seen how each of us may have a most secure or personally comprehensible starting point: thoughts, feelings, body or behaviour. And from this we describe and experience our distressed selves, and then make contact with others when seeking explanation or relief. So this is then picked up, processed and reflected by the different modes and styles of therapy: each engages, explains or attempts to evoke change through a primary channel – either thoughts, or feelings, or behaviour, or the body.

D: Can you give me some examples?

Yes, but only very briefly here. We may, for example, be preoccupied by obsessive thoughts, or overwhelmed by frightening or bleak feelings, or troubled by unaccountable behaviours or physical symptoms. Any of these can dominate our consciousness in a way that seems autonomous and unmoveable – as if they have a life of their own that pushes much else aside. Naturally we seek mode-specific help for our disturbed thoughts, or feelings, or behaviour, or physical dis-ease.

Yet what we may be failing to see is that we are all much more complicated than this, and that these different modes are only separate in our mind's schemes and preferences... so this determines our experience of how and where we get stuck! In reality, if we change any one of these aspects it will usually change any, or all, of the others. *If I change how I think, I change how I feel, I change what I do and my experience of my body:* we can rearrange that into any other sequence and it will be equally true. That's Holism: that's something professionals have recently attempted to capture, reinstate and commodify by calling it Integrative Psychotherapy – effectively another brand name for putting Humpty Dumpty (Psychotherapy) back together again... after we've made such a thorough job of fragmenting it. That's what Figure 2 here illustrates.

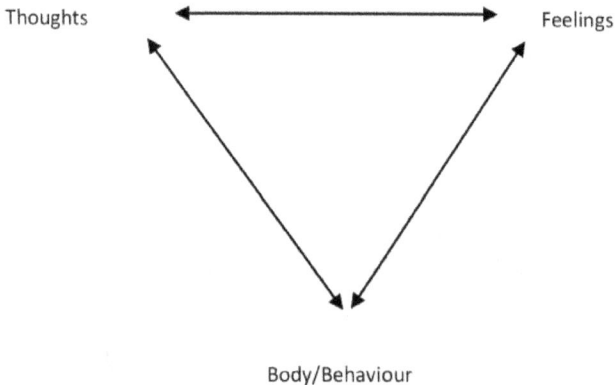

Figure 2: 'Real Life'. Holism and Integrative Psychotherapy

*D: So why **has** psychotherapy divided into ever more varieties?*

Well, partly for effective reasons, partly not.

It's often most helpful to start on the other person's 'home territory', offering them a 'specialist' symptoms-based approach. But there is a paradox and caveat here because – importantly – it may later be the more effective part of healing and growth to venture into new territory, where the person is, initially, *least* familiar and comfortable.

A second reason is that therapists – like everybody else – have their favourite modes of experience and explanation, so this is how they will choose to engage and theorise with others. This can become problematic if the therapist is grandiose or power-hungry, for they will then aggrandise their preference, their comfort-zone, into a scheme that assumes command and primacy for others – such are the specious and dangerous panaceas we can offer one another.

And then there are more commonplace – now cultural – modi operandi of packaging, commodification and marketisation: certainly, in our contemporary world, we need brand-distinction, niche-definition and a guise of exclusivity. You can't claim these while appealing also for Holism and flexibility.

D: Holism?

Yes, our due attention to the mystery of how the whole is more than the sum of its parts. That's not helped by how – as we've seen – therapists themselves often increase fragmentation and boundaries. All this fragmentation is probably due, too, to therapists' all-too-human needs to have 'ownership' of defined territory that they feel they command and can mark as their own: 'defensible space' … a kind of land enclosure.

The last reason I can think of is an important expansion of this last point. It returns to the theme so central to our long discussion here: how we humans take fright at our own complexity; how we often need to contain and confine our world to secure a sense of safety and anchorage … to console ourselves with boundaries and finitude…

D: Back to my Planet Earth, please! A very practical question: who is psychotherapy suitable for?

I'm afraid my answer may be a bit less practical: I won't give you a diagnostic list, but can suggest some principles. Firstly, psychotherapy is unlikely to offer a quick-fix for any of the kind of human problems we have described. Also, it can only 'work' with those problems when a person can tolerate questions, ambiguities and other perspectives that may depart far from the terra firma of usual presumptions. These risks, and trust, are necessary for the 'human induction' we have talked about to occur.

So we can see how any comfort, healing and growth induced by psychotherapy will need a basis of our courage, curiosity and candour. Our existential anxieties cannot be simply 'fixed' by conductive treatments; our healing inductions require from us more time and patience…

D: So what are the possible effects of these 'inductions' then?

Well, when these things are invested and then evolve together, then many kinds of problems – physical, mental or spiritual – may be beneficently influenced.

D: That's very vague. What, specifically, do you mean?

Sometimes a transformation/disappearance of tribulations occurs; more commonly our attitude changes to what we can do, and what we must endure. In physical illnesses, psychotherapy's inductive approaches will often help the conductive medical treatments to work better – these different approaches then become not just complementary, but synergistic. This is true, too, of severe mental illness although here the more formal and 'denser' forms of psychotherapy may be better dispersed to lighter, more flexible psychotherapeutic influences.

Beneath all this, though, is the simple guiding principle: is the person interested and open to such challenge and change, such seeing beyond the familiar: *metanoia*. What are they on for?

D: But can it ever be harmful?

No, not if this principle is respected. Any harm would come from a therapist's vanity, hubris, or worse.

D: Ugh! You seem to be finishing with yet another paradox and ambiguity!

Yes, human struggles and troubles are sometimes not what or where they seem.

You can take a horse to water, but you can't make him drink.

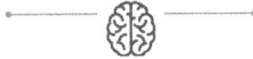

Glad Day, William Blake 1794

Chapter Eleven:
First and last words:
from God to Human

And God saw everything that he had made and, behold, it was very good.

Genesis 1

Ring the bells that still can ring

Forget your perfect offering

There is a crack in everything

That's how the light gets in.

Leonard Cohen (1992) Anthem

Appendix:
Notes and Acknowledgements

It is said that there have been no radically new ideas since the ancient Greek philosophers.

So, this brief but very wide-spanned book is bound to sit on the shoulders of many erstwhile thinkers and writers. Most originality here is merely in the framing and presentation, not in the elemental ideas themselves.

The ideas that have been borrowed and patterned here are so variously sourced and so numerous that any attempt to list them comprehensively would massively out-bulk the main text with mere references, so I have not attempted this. Nevertheless, a very brief list of the erstwhile writers I have here been most consciously indebted to are: Emil Durkheim, Erich Fromm, Eric Berne, Jerome Frank, Viktor Frankl and, most recently, Yuval Noah Harari. All their ideas have been fashioned to suit my own arguments, so any acknowledged plagiarism may also be accused of inaccuracy. Also, I am aware that these mentoring writers themselves sat on others' shoulders.

What I have offered here, therefore, is a broad-brushed philosophical piece engaging a very wide scope and then condensed to a brevity that some will find impudent. In this spirit I have not only foregone a schematised bibliography, but have also abstained from extensive academic references for assertions about mental illness, morbidity statistics, psychotherapy research, ethology, evolutionary psychology... and so forth. The choice and style is for brevity and readability, not academic inviolability or inclusion.

Who else to thank? Well, my ideas come, in large part, also from decades of conversations with fellow humans all trying to make, or secure, sense for our lives: in work with colleagues and designated sufferers, in my private space with good friends and loved ones. Any list would be another that becomes encyclopaedic, so too long to be readable or useful.

Particular and pragmatic, yet certainly personal, thanks though are due for technical help with this book: to Olivia Eisinger and Chris Day at Filament Publishing for their friendly guidance, advice and effectiveness; to Jacki Reason for her patient deciphering of my complex and pedantic handwritten notebooks and then typing and launching them into the 21st century. Without them all, this book would have remained merely as swarming and fermenting thoughts.

It would have remained….. not here.

The Author

David Zigmond trained in medicine, psychiatry and psychotherapy and has served as a frontline NHS doctor for fifty years. His educational work, blogs and many publications about healthcare draw from this experience, as does his anthology *If You Want Good Personal Healthcare, See A Vet: Industrialised Humanity: Why and how should we care for one another?*

His work as a psychotherapist, together with healthcare education, writing and activism, continues in London.

More on his other books can be found at

davidzigmond.org.uk

Many of his articles are on his Archive site.

www.marco-learningsystems.com/pages/david-zigmond/ david-zigmond.html

Email: *zigmond@jackireason.co.uk*

Why Do We Suffer?

Do we pay an inescapable price for our humanity?

What and who can help?

And How Do We Heal?